A Kid's Guide to Drawing the Presidents of the United States of America™

How to Draw the Life and Times of
William Howard Taft

Ryan P. Randolph

The Rosen Publishing Group's
PowerKids Press™
New York

To my father, William Randolph

Published in 2006 by The Rosen Publishing Group, Inc.
29 East 21st Street, New York, NY 10010

First Edition

Editor: Rachel O'Connor
Layout Design: Elana Davidian
Photo Researcher: Amy Feinberg

Illustrations: All illustrations by Holly Cefrey.
Photo Credits: p. 4 The Art Archive/Culver Pictures; pp. 7, 16 © Bettmann/Corbis; pp. 8, 18 William Howard Taft National Historic Site, National Park Service; p. 9 © 2005 University of Cincinnati Fine Arts Collection; p. 10 © Yale University; p. 12 Rutherford B. Hayes Presidential Center; pp. 14, 26 Library of Congress Prints and Photographs Division; p. 20 Roger-Viollet, Paris/Bridgeman Art Library; p. 22 Ohio Historical Society; p. 24 Courtesy of the James David Preston illustrated autograph book, 1904–1924 in the Archives of American Art, Smithsonian Institution; p. 28 White House Historical Association (White House Collection).

Library of Congress Cataloging-in-Publication Data

Randolph, Ryan P.
   How to draw the life and times of William Howard Taft / Ryan P. Randolph.— 1st ed.
      p. cm. — (A kid's guide to drawing the presidents of the United States of America)
   Includes index.
   ISBN 1-4042-3003-3 (lib. bdg.)
   1. Taft, William H. (William Howard), 1857–1930—Juvenile literature. 2. Presidents—United States—Biography—Juvenile literature. 3. Judges–United States—Biography—Juvenile literature. 4. United States. Supreme Court—Biography—Juvenile literature. 5. Drawing—Technique—Juvenile literature. I. Title. II. Series.
   E762.R36 2006
   973.91'2'092—dc22

                                   2005002887

Printed in China

Contents

Meet William Howard Taft

William Howard Taft served as the twenty-seventh president of the United States from 1909 to 1913. Taft is best known as the only person in the history of the United States to serve as both the president of the United States and as the chief justice of the United States. The chief justice  is the head of the Supreme Court. Taft was often known as Big Bill Taft because of his large frame. He had a good sense of humor, and he was an honest, generous, and loving person.

Taft enjoyed his work as chief justice more than his duties as president. Although Taft was a very good judge and administrator, he was not a strong leader. He did not like politics and conflict with others. He once wrote, "Politics, when I'm in it, makes me sick."

Taft was born on September 15, 1857, in Cincinnati, Ohio, to Louisa and Alphonso Taft. The Tafts were a wealthy family that expected a lot of their children. William went to school in Cincinnati until he was ready to study at Yale University, which he did in 1874. Then he went on to Cincinnati Law School. After graduating and becoming a lawyer, Taft followed in his father's footsteps and rose through the ranks of the Republican Party in Ohio. He was appointed as a federal judge at the age of 34.

While serving as a judge, Taft was asked by President William McKinley to become the governor of the Philippine Islands in 1901. After consulting with his wife, Nellie, Taft took the job. During his time in the Philippines, Taft proved his skills at administration by setting up the country's legal and governmental systems.

You will need the following supplies to draw the life and times of William Howard Taft:

✓ A sketch pad   ✓ An eraser   ✓ A pencil   ✓ A ruler

These are some of the shapes and drawing terms you need to know:

Horizontal Line	——	Squiggly Line	
Oval	⬭	Trapezoid	
Rectangle	▭	Triangle	△
Shading		Vertical Line	|
Slanted Line	/	Wavy Line	

The Presidency of William Howard Taft

Theodore Roosevelt, who became president in 1901, respected the work his friend Taft was doing in the Philippines. He made Taft the secretary of war. Then, in 1908, Roosevelt encouraged Taft to run for president. Taft did not want to be president, but Roosevelt and Nellie Taft convinced him to run.

Taft won the election. However, Taft's presidency soon became caught up in scandals. This happened because of Taft's choice of advisers. It also had to do with his support of a law that increased tariffs, or taxes on foreign goods. Roosevelt became dissatisfied with Taft's presidency. In the election of 1912, the one-time friends ran against each other, splitting the Republican Party voters into two groups. The split led to the victory of the democratic candidate, Woodrow Wilson.

Taft was relieved not to be president for another term. He became a professor at Yale in 1913. In 1921, Taft received the opportunity he had always wanted. President Warren G. Harding appointed him chief justice of the United States.

William Howard Taft campaigns for reelection in the 1912 presidential election. During his first and only term as president, Taft continued some of Roosevelt's policies. He also brought in his own laws to improve the organization of the federal budget and civil service.

Taft's Ohio

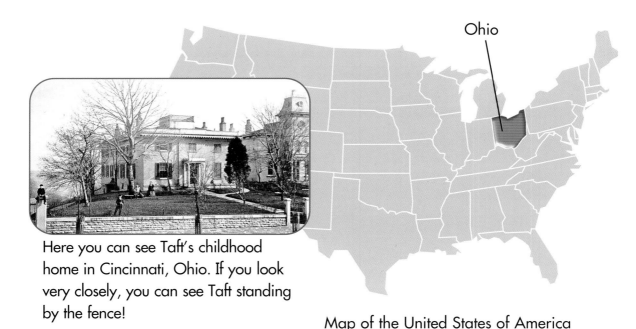

Here you can see Taft's childhood home in Cincinnati, Ohio. If you look very closely, you can see Taft standing by the fence!

Ohio

Map of the United States of America

Ohio is sometimes called the Mother of Presidents because eight presidents, including William Howard Taft, were from the Buckeye State. Taft was raised in Cincinnati, Ohio. When he was growing up, his family lived in the Mount Auburn section of Cincinnati. At the time Mount Auburn was considered a suburb of Cincinnati, where many of the city's wealthy people lived in large houses. Today, however, Taft's birthplace is found in the busy center of Cincinnati, in what is now a less wealthy part of the city. The house is part of the William Taft National Historic Site. Four of the rooms have been restored to how they looked in the nineteenth century. The second floor holds an exhibit honoring Taft's accomplishments. There is also a small museum, called the Taft Education Center, next to the house. The education center contains a robotic figure of Charlie Taft, President Taft's son. The robotic Charlie Taft tells stories of his father and other family members.

People can visit a statue of Taft on the grounds of the University of Cincinnati, where the William Howard Taft Memorial can be found. The Cincinnati Law School, where Taft went to school, is now part of the university.

The William Howard Taft Memorial is a bronze statue of Taft that commemorates, or remembers, his service as chief justice of the United States. The statue is more than 7 feet (2 m) high and nearly 3 feet (1 m) wide. It shows Taft holding a book. He is in his judicial robe as chief justice.

Childhood and Education

William Howard Taft was born on September 15, 1857. His parents were Louisa Torrey Taft and Alphonso Taft. Alphonso Taft was a successful judge and lawyer in Cincinnati. Alphonso had served as the secretary of war and attorney general for President Ulysses S. Grant. William Taft had two half brothers, Charles and Peter, from Alphonso's first marriage. Taft also had two younger brothers and a younger sister.

Taft was always big as a child, but he was also tall and strong. He was known for having a good sense of humor. Taft did well in school, and in 1874 he headed east to Yale University in New Haven, Connecticut. At Yale, Taft often procrastinated, or put off doing his schoolwork, until the last minute. He still graduated in 1878, ranking second in his class. Taft then decided to come home to attend the Cincinnati Law School that fall. While he was in law school, Taft took a part-time job as a reporter for the *Cincinnati Commercial*, where he continued to work until shortly after he graduated in 1880.

1

Let's draw the Yale University shield. You can begin by drawing a circle. Inside the circle draw the shield as shown. Be sure to draw the shield in the center of the circle.

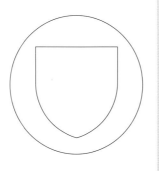

2

Inside the shield draw a rectangle. Add a vertical line down the center of the rectangle. This is your guide for the book. Next draw curved shapes at the top and bottom edges of the circle. These are banners. The one on the top is longer than the one on the bottom.

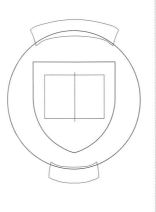

3

Erase any extra lines. Draw the ends of the banners as shown. Begin to draw the leaves at the bottom of the circle. Add the words "LUX" and "YALE" inside the banners. Draw curvy lines for the book pages. Add a small curved line under the rectangle.

4

Erase extra lines. Add more leaves. Add lines inside the leaves you drew in step 4. Add short, slightly curved lines to the ends of the banners. Add the letters "ET" in the top banner. Add more pages to the book. Draw curvy lines that look like hooks at the sides of the book.

5

Erase any extra lines. Add more lines inside the remaining leaves. Add writing inside the pages of the book as shown. Add details to the sides of the book. Draw two small lines connecting the pages at the bottom. Write the word "VERITAS" in the top banner.

6

Finish your drawing with shading. Start by coloring in the area behind the book inside the shield. Next you can lightly shade the edges of the book. That's it. You are finished. "LUX ET VERITAS" means "light and truth" in Latin.

Political Appointments

In October 1881, William Howard Taft was appointed to be the assistant prosecutor, or lawyer, for Hamilton County. Hamilton is the county in which Cincinnati is located. This was the beginning of Taft's long career in public service.

In 1882, President Chester A. Arthur appointed young Taft as a collector of internal revenue, because of his father's service to the Republican Party. Taft did not like parts of the job, such as being asked to fire some members of his staff. In 1883, Taft quit and opened up his own private law practice. He worked there until 1887, when he was appointed to be a judge in the Cincinnati Superior Court, shown here.

Taft's reputation in the Republican Party grew. In 1890, President Benjamin Harrison made Taft solicitor general of the United States. Taft and his wife, Nellie, whom he had married in 1886, moved to Washington, D.C. It was during this time that Taft met and became friends with a young Harvard graduate named Theodore Roosevelt.

1

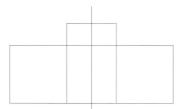

Let's draw the Cincinnati Superior Court. Today it is called Hamilton County Courthouse. Begin by drawing a horizontal rectangle. Draw a vertical rectangle on top of it. Add a vertical line down the center of the vertical rectangle.

2

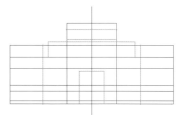

Draw five horizontal lines going across the horizontal rectangle. Some of these lines will serve as guides for windows.

3

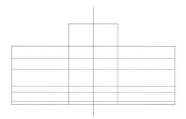

Draw a door. Draw a horizontal line with two vertical lines at each end. Add two horizontal lines and two vertical lines to the building.

4

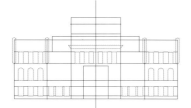

Begin drawing the windows. Notice how some windows have arches at their tops. Draw the trapezoid in the middle section of the building as shown. Draw four columns along the top of the building.

5

Erase extra lines. Add lines to the tops of the columns. Draw two shapes coming from the innermost columns. Add more windows. Add details to the windows you drew in step 4. Add an arch and more lines to the entrance.

6

Erase the center guideline and any extra lines. Add more windows and arches. Looking carefully at the drawing, add more details to the building as shown.

7

Erase extra lines. Draw more arches above some of the windows. Add columns in the door. Add more details to the windows and the rest of the building.

8

Erase extra lines. You can add as much detail to your drawing as you would like. Finish with shading. Well done.

Taft and Labor Unions

In 1892, Taft accepted an appointment as a judge on the Sixth Federal Circuit Court of Appeals. Taft knew that experience as an appeals court judge

might one day lead to a position on the Supreme Court. Taft was at his happiest when deciding how to interpret the law as a judge.

During this time there was a great deal of unrest between men who worked at railroad, steel, or mining companies and the owners of these businesses. Companies often paid workers too little or made them work in unsafe conditions. Sometimes workers staged fierce protests, which were often illegal. Taft believed in the fair treatment of workers but not in the workers' right to strike. For example, to solve one labor problem Taft ordered other railroads to carry the freight, or loads, of a railroad company whose workers were on strike. By refusing to allow other railroad workers to strike, Taft stopped the original railroad strike. This made him unpopular with unions.

1

Taft was unpopular with railroad unions. You are now going to draw a picture of a train from that period of time. Start by drawing a tube as shown.

2

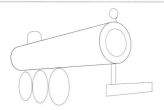

Draw three ovals for wheels. Draw the curved shape on top of the train. Draw the small circle and curved line near the front on top. This is the light. Add an oval inside the end of the tube. Draw the straight lines extending from the tube to form the shapes shown.

3

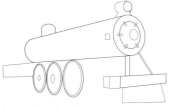

Add details to the light. Draw more ovals inside the wheels. Add details to the front of the tube shape. Draw an arch on the side. Draw straight lines at the back and front of the train.

4

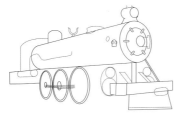

Erase extra lines. Draw lines going across the wheels. Draw the shapes on the back. Looking carefully at the drawing, add the shapes on the top, side, and front of the train.

5

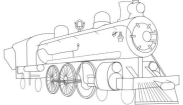

Erase extra lines. Add the new shapes to the top of the train. Draw lines at the back. Draw the long line that goes across the side of the train and curves into the front. Draw more lines at the front of the train and at the side by the wheels.

6

Erase extra lines. Add more lines to the bell on the top of the train. Add details to the side of the train. Add spokes to two of the wheels. Add more wheels. Add extra lines to the front of the train.

7

Draw smoke at the top. Add windows at the back. Draw more spokes and circles inside the wheels. Add any remaining details as shown.

8

Erase extra lines. Finish your drawing with shading. Notice how the shading is darker in some parts than in others.

Nellie Taft

As a judge Taft worked fairly and according to his interpretation of the law. At times Taft shared his private opinions to his closest adviser, his wife, Nellie. Throughout his career, Taft would rarely make a decision without consulting Nellie, and Nellie constantly pushed Taft to greater heights in his career.

Helen "Nellie" Herron was from a well-known Cincinnati family. Taft first got to know Nellie when he began attending a literary salon she organized. A literary salon is a meeting in which people socialize and talk about books, politics, and daily events. Taft courted the charming, ambitious, and educated Nellie, and they were married in June 1886.

The Tafts had three children, Robert Alphonso, Helen, and Charles Phelps. In the summers the Taft family vacationed in Murray Bay, Quebec, which is on the St. Lawrence River in Canada. His time as a judge on the court of appeals, with his family and vacation home, was a happy one for Taft.

1

It's time to draw Nellie Taft. Start by drawing a rectangle. This will be your frame for the portrait, or picture. Inside the rectangle draw a guide oval for the head. Draw straight guidelines for the neck, shoulders, and arms.

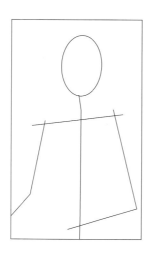

2

Draw a curve for the side of the head. Draw an oval for the ear. Draw guidelines for the eyes, nose, and mouth. Add lines for the neck and shoulders. Draw a large oval guide for the hand.

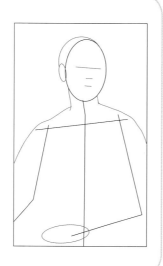

3 Erase extra lines. Draw a long wavy line for the outline of the hair. Add the hairline at the front of the head and at the top of the ear. Draw the inside of the ear. Draw the eyes, nose, and mouth. Draw the cheek and jawline. Add lines for the clothes. Draw part of the wrist and thumb.

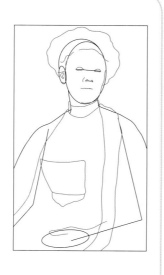

4

Erase extra lines. Add lines for waves in the hair. Draw earrings. Add details as shown to the face. Add details to the necklace you started in the last step. Add lines to the front of the dress as shown. Add lines and shapes to the wrap. Add curvy lines for the finger.

5

Erase extra lines. Finish off the eyes and chin. Add tiny circles to the necklace. Draw the wavy lines on the front of the dress. Add the design, or shapes, to the border of the wrap. Add lines for folds in the skirt part of the dress.

6

You can add as much detail as you would like. Look at the photograph on the opposite page to help you. Finish with shading. You can make the background dark. Notice that the shading is darker in some areas. You are finished. Well done!

Governor of the Philippines

From his happy post as a judge, Taft was surprised by a request in 1900 from President William McKinley. He asked Taft to serve as the president of the Second

Philippine Commission. In 1898, the United States had fought the Spanish-American War. As a result of the treaty that ended the war, the United States came into possession of the Philippine Islands in the Pacific Ocean. McKinley wanted Taft to serve as governor and organize a civilian government there. After talking about the appointment with Nellie, Taft accepted the job. In his new role, Taft proved to be a capable manager and administrator. He created a new system of laws and rules for the Philippines.

Both Nellie and Taft were treated like royalty on the islands, and they became fond of the Filipino people. In 1905, the people of the Philippines presented him with a key to Manila, shown above. Manila is the capital of the Philippines. The key stands for the great respect the people had for the work Taft did there.

1

Begin by drawing a trapezoid. Inside the trapezoid draw the long shape as shown. Notice how the ends of this shape are curved.

2

Draw another trapezoid outside the one you just drew. Add curvy and straight lines to the long shape. This is the start of the key. Add the shape to the left to begin the handle of the key.

3

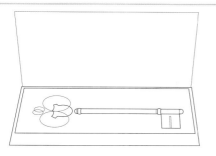

Add the lid of the box using straight lines. Draw a thin rectangle on the end of the key. Add curvy lines to the body of the key. Draw two ovals on the handle of the key. Add two smaller ovals that overlap.

4

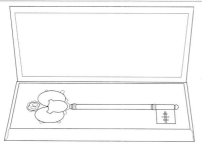

Erase extra lines. Add a trapezoid inside the box lid. Draw two wavy lines on the bottom corners of the box. Add details to the key as shown.

5

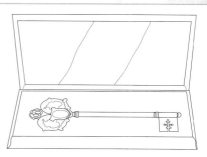

Erase extra lines. Draw two long wavy lines inside the lid. Add two small curved lines near the bottom corners of the lid. Add two little rectangles to the end of the key. Add more details to the handle of the key as shown.

6

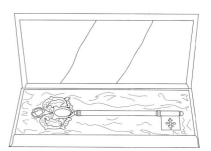

Erase extra lines. Draw squiggly lines inside the box. This is for the folds in the material below the key. Finish off the details to the handle of the key as shown.

7

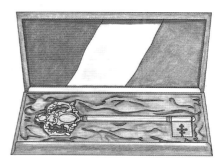

Finish your drawing with shading. Notice how the middle stripe in the lid is white. Well done. You did a great job!

Secretary of War

Theodore Roosevelt, who was Taft's friend from his days as solicitor general, had become a hero in the Spanish-American War. He became President McKinley's

vice president. When McKinley was assassinated, or killed, in 1901, Roosevelt became president. Ever popular with the voters, he was reelected in 1904.

Roosevelt made Taft secretary of war in 1905. As secretary of war, Taft needed to travel a lot. One of his jobs was to oversee the construction of the Panama Canal in Central America. The canal, shown here, was being built to shorten the route between the Pacific Ocean and the Atlantic Ocean. In 1905, while Russia was at war with Japan, Taft was sent to notify the Japanese that the United States wanted to remain at peace in Asia. In 1906, Taft rushed to Cuba as a show of support to the government in the face of a revolution by the Cuban people. Roosevelt depended on Taft as his adviser in foreign affairs. He thought that Taft might be ready for even higher political office.

1

Let's start our boat by drawing a large curve as shown. Draw a straight line across the bottom of the curve.

2

Draw another curve around the first one you drew in step 1, only make it longer. Draw the shape inside the curve. This is the start of the cabin.

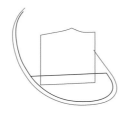

3

Draw another curve along the bottom of the boat. Draw horizontal lines across the cabin. Add curved lines for one side of the roof as shown. Add a slanted line to the right of the cabin.

4

Erase extra lines. Draw the other side of the roof. Draw a vertical line for the flagpole. Draw a semicircle above the boat. Add details to the boat and the cabin as shown.

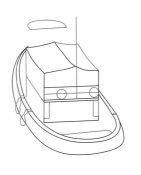

5

Erase extra lines. Add a flag to the pole. Draw a small line at the top. Draw a smokestack on the boat. Add straight lines to the smokestack. Add details to the boat and cabin. Draw wavy lines for ripples in the water.

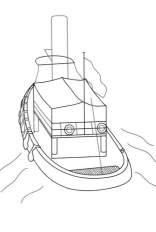

6

Erase extra lines. Add another flagpole at one end of the boat. Add a small flag to the pole you drew in step 5. Add details to the flag you drew before. Add details to the smokestack and to the cabin. Add more ripples.

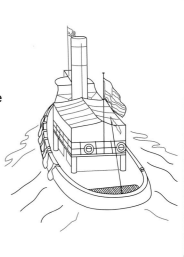

7

Erase extra lines. Finish your drawing with shading. You can make your drawing darker in some parts as shown. Well done! You did a super job.

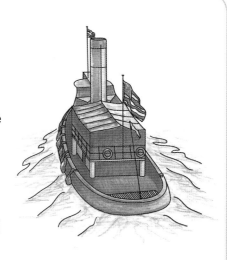

An Unwilling President

In 1904, Roosevelt announced that he would not run in the election of 1908. Instead Roosevelt supported Taft to be president, so Taft could carry on his policies. With the encouragement of Nellie and his brothers, and of course the backing of Roosevelt, Taft won the presidential election of 1908. One of the most challenging issues during Taft's presidency was that of tariff reform. Many Republicans supported high tariffs on foreign goods. Tariffs were good for U.S. businesses but not for working people. As U.S. businesses became more successful, some Republicans, like Taft, felt tariffs should be lowered. Then more people would benefit from America's success. Taft called a meeting of Congress in 1909 to reduce tariffs. Instead, Congress created a bill that raised tariffs in general, while reducing tariffs on just a few things. Taft felt the change was better than nothing and supported the Payne-Aldrich Tariff. Unfortunately for Taft, many felt the bill was a sellout of his campaign promise, and his popularity suffered.

1

You are going to draw part of Taft's election campaign poster. Start by drawing a circle. Draw a vertical line down the center. Draw a horizontal line across the bottom of the vertical line.

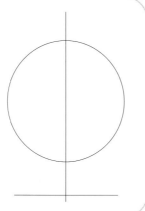

2

Draw two sets of slanted lines that cross over each other to make an X shape. Draw circles on the tops of these lines. These are poles. Draw slanted lines between the poles.

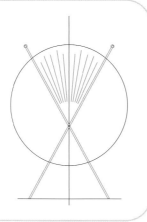

3 Erase extra lines. Draw curvy lines for flags coming from the poles. Draw shapes at the tops of the poles. These will be little birds. Draw a shield between the poles. Draw flowers at the bottom of the circle.

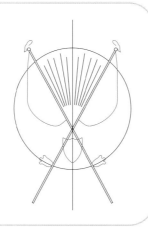

4 Erase extra lines. Finish the birds on the poles. Draw stars on the flags. Begin to add the wings, neck, and legs of the eagle coming from the shield. Add an oval for the head. Add details to the flowers.

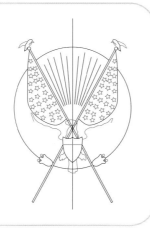

5

Erase extra lines. Add more flowers around the edge of the circle. Draw stars and vertical lines inside the shield. Add the wavy shape below the eagle. Add lines inside the head oval. Draw the rest of the eagle as shown.

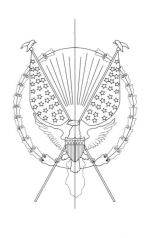

6

Erase extra lines. Add two more flowers at the bottom. Add an eye and a line to the beak on the eagle. Draw squiggly lines around the eagle as shown. Those are the stripes on the flags. Don't forget the curved lines above the eagle's head.

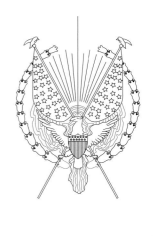

7

You have nearly finished. All that is left to do is to add some shading. See where the shading is lighter in some parts. Notice that the stars in the flags are left white. Good job.

A Break with Roosevelt

As president, Taft faced several scandals including accusations of dishonesty that caused him anxiety and a drop in popularity within the Republican Party. The

combination of Taft's weak leadership and the tariff bill mess led to a steep drop in Taft's support. Roosevelt became so dissatisfied with Taft that he decided to run again for president, against his old friend.

In the election of 1912, the Republican Party was divided between Taft and Roosevelt supporters. Taft supporters liked things the way they were. Roosevelt Republicans supported change. They wanted to put limitations on businesses that would benefit working people and conserve land for future generations. Taft did not like being president, and he did not enjoy the conflict with his friend. However, he felt he had to run to stop Roosevelt from taking America in a wrong direction. In the end the Democratic candidate, Woodrow Wilson, won the election easily.

1 The cartoon shows the split between Taft and Theodore Roosevelt, or "Teddy," as he is called in the cartoon. Draw a circle for the man's belly. Draw an oval for the head. Draw lines for the legs and arms.

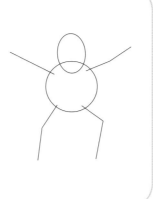

2 Draw guides for the eyes, nose, and mouth. Draw ovals and circles as guides for the arms, hands, legs, knees, and feet.

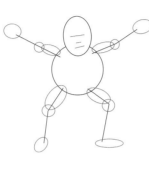

3 Using the guides you drew in the last step, draw outlines of the arms, body, and legs. Draw the hat. Add circles for the eyes. Draw the nose and mouth, too. Begin the hands as shown.

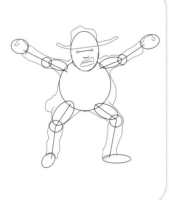

4 Erase extra lines. Finish off the hands. Add the ears. Add lines to the face. Draw the jacket lines. Add a curved line around the belly. Add lines to the pants. Add lines for the shoes.

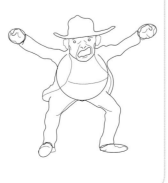

5 Erase extra lines. Draw the lines with curving tops that he is holding in his hands. Add lines for wrinkles in the hat. Add lines to the ears and nose. Draw more lines on the belly and on his shirt. Add more lines to the shoes.

6 Erase extra lines. Draw wrinkles on his jacket and pants. Draw flags at the tops of the lines you drew in step 5. Write the names "TAFT" and "TEDDY" on either side as shown. Finish his shoes.

7 Finish your cartoon with shading. Make it lighter in some parts and darker in others. That's it. You're finished.

Chief Justice of the Supreme Court

After losing the election, Taft was relieved to return to a more private life. He soon took a job as a professor at Yale in 1913. In 1921, Taft finally received the call he had always wanted. President Warren G. Harding appointed Taft chief justice of the United States. Taft worked hard and was very happy. The inside of the Supreme Court, where Taft worked, is shown above.

Under Taft the Supreme Court ruled on cases that supported the amendment banning alcohol and the new law that established an income tax. Overall Taft's Supreme Court did not rule on any major historical cases. However, he did make a lasting improvement to the federal court system through his administrative skills.

Taft's work slowed after he experienced some heart problems in 1924. His health continued to fail, and he was hospitalized in 1929. Taft retired from the Supreme Court on February 3, 1930. He died a little more than a month later on March 8, 1930.

1

You are drawing the inside of the Supreme Court. Draw a big rectangle. Draw a rectangle inside it. Draw a line down the center.

2

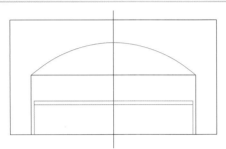

Draw a curved line across the top of the small rectangle. Draw two vertical lines and two horizontal lines inside the small rectangle.

3

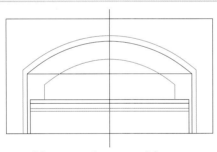

Draw vertical lines with curved lines connecting the tops. Draw two horizontal lines.

4

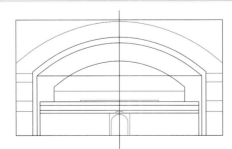

Draw a large curve across the top. Add more horizontal lines to your drawing. Draw an arch and straight lines at the bottom. Add a small shape above these lines.

5

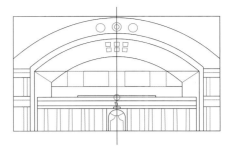

Erase extra lines. Draw the circles and squares at the top as shown. Look carefully at the drawing. You have a lot of straight lines to draw. Do the best you can. Add the details to the center section as shown.

6

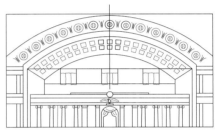

Erase extra lines. Add more circles to the top. Add the rest of the details to finish the design. Draw more small rectangles in the row below. Add details to the windows. Draw wings on the eagle. Add details to the columns at the bottom. Finish the arched shape.

7

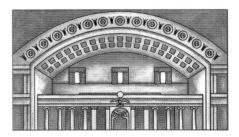

Erase extra lines. Finish your drawing of the Supreme Court with shading. Some parts are dark. Some are light.

Taft's Legacy

From his days as a prosecutor and judge in Cincinnati to his work on the Supreme Court, Taft proved to be an able public servant. As president, Taft had some notable accomplishments, including his superior administrative skills. He was the first president to propose that the U.S. government create a federal budget to oversee spending. After 1920, Warren G. Harding made this practice into law. Taft also pushed Congress to tax corporations. Through his attorney general George Wickersham, he used the courts to break up corporations that became too large. In addition, Taft supported laws that controlled railroad fare hikes to protect passengers.

Taft's generous spirit, his dislike of conflict, and his good humor are what he is remembered for. He is not thought of as one of the most important presidents. However, to this day, William Howard Taft remains the only person to serve as both president and chief justice of the United States.

1

It is time to draw Taft. Draw a rectangle. Next draw an oval for the head. Draw a center guideline that is slightly slanted. Add more straight guides for the shoulders and arms. Draw ovals for the hands.

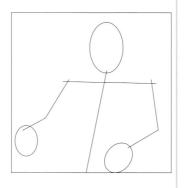

2

Draw a curve and an oval for the side of the head and the ear. Draw guidelines for the eyes, nose, and mouth as shown. Use the guidelines you drew in the last step to draw the outline of the shoulders and arms.

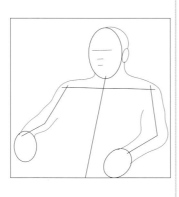

3

Erase extra lines. Use the face guides to draw the eyes, eyebrows, and nose. Draw the line for the cheek and chin. Add a line to his ear. Draw the collar of his shirt. Draw the hands as shown. Draw the squiggly line in the bottom right corner. This is part of the chair.

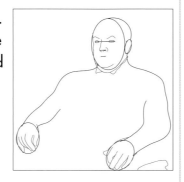

4

Erase extra lines. Draw lines for the hair. Draw lids on the eyes. Draw lines inside the ear. Draw the curly moustache. Draw the jacket and tie. Add a line below his hand for part of the chair.

5

Erase extra lines. Finish the eyes. Draw the bottom lip. Draw a small vertical line on the chin. Add a small shape below the ear for hair. Draw the vest and cuffs. Draw lines for wrinkles in his jacket. Add the line where the sleeve and the chair meet.

6

Erase extra lines. You can finish your drawing with shading. Notice which parts are darker than others. Well done! You did a really super job.

Timeline

1857   William Howard Taft is born in Cincinnati, Ohio, on September 15.

1878   Taft graduates from Yale University.

1880   Taft graduates from Cincinnati Law School.

1881–1887   Taft works as a lawyer.

1887–1890   Taft is appointed as a superior court judge for Cincinnati.

1890–1892   Taft serves as U.S. solicitor general.

1892–1900   Taft serves as a judge on the U.S. Sixth Circuit Court of Appeals.

1900   Taft is appointed as the president of the Second Philippine Commission.

1901–1904   Taft serves as the governor of the Philippines. Taft improves the country's educational, legal, and public transportation systems. He also works to establish some self-government.

1905–1908   Taft serves as the U.S. secretary of war under President Roosevelt.

1908   Taft is elected the twenty-seventh president of the United States.

1909   The Payne-Aldrich Tariff Bill is passed.

1912   Taft loses his presidential reelection campaign. Democrat Woodrow Wilson wins.

1913   Taft becomes a law professor at Yale University.

1921   Taft is appointed chief justice of the United States by President Warren G. Harding.

1930   Taft retires from the Supreme Court on February 3, and dies on March 8.

Glossary

administrator (ed-MIH-nih-stray-ter) One who directs or manages something.

amendment (uh-MEND-ment) An addition or a change to the Constitution.

attorney general (uh-TUR-nee JEN-rul) Chief law officer and legal counsel of the government of a state or nation.

budget (BUH-jit) A plan to spend a certain amount of money in a period of time.

chief justice (CHEEF JUS-tus) The head judge of a high court having several judges.

Congress (KON-gres) The branch of the U.S. government that makes laws.

foreign (FOR-in) Outside one's own country.

internal revenue (in-TUR-nul REH-veh-noo) A government department that collects taxes.

interpret (in-TER-pret) To explain the meaning and purpose of.

lawyer (LOY-er) A person who gives advice about the law.

legacy (LEH-guh-see) Something left behind by a person's actions.

policies (PAH-lih-seez) Laws that people use to help them make decisions.

reform (rih-FORM) Change or improvement.

Republican Party (rih-PUH-blih-ken PAR-tee) One of the two major U.S. political parties.

reputation (reh-pyoo-TAY-shun) The ideas people have about another person.

restored (rih-STORD) Put back, returned to an earlier state.

revolution (reh-vuh-LOO-shun) A complete change in government.

scandals (SKAN-dulz) Conduct that people find shocking and bad.

secretary of war (SEH-kruh-ter-ee UV WOR) Former member of the president's cabinet of advisers. The secretary of war dealt with military and foreign affairs.

site (SYT) The place where a certain event happens.

solicitor general (seh-LIH-seh-ter JEN-rul) An appointed law officer assisting an attorney general.

suburb (SUH-berb) An area of homes and businesses that is near a large city.

Supreme Court (suh–PREEM KORT) The highest court in the nation.

tariffs (TER-ufs) Taxes on foreign goods.

treaty (TREE-tee) An official agreement, signed and agreed upon by each party.

Index

Web Sites

Due to the changing nature of Internet links, PowerKids Press has developed an online list of Web sites related to the subject of this book. This site is updated regularly. Please use this link to access the list:

www.powerkidslinks.com/kgdpusa/taft/

DUE DATE

			Printed in USA